Ball Pythons

Written by Jessica Lee Anderson
Photos by David Kenny

Paperback ISBN: 978-1-964078-31-1

To Trasi Judd, a wealth of knowledge, kindness, and compassion! I can't recommend A NEW KEEPER'S GUIDE TO BALL PYTHONS enough! - JLA

To Peter and Edel Kenny and Mike and Sue LoRusso. - DK

We would like to thank the following:

Hudson Valley Reptile & Rescue: A reptile rescuer and educator, Brian Parkhurst has been passing on his knowledge of reptiles through educational programs for 22 years. Brian works hard to find homes for reptiles that are surrendered to the rescue. HVR&R is located in Saugerties, New York. https://www.hvreptilerescue.org

Ocean Gallery II Fish and Reptiles: A small, local, family operated pet store in North Plainfield, New Jersey, run by Craig Ost who has over 30 years of experience in reptile keeping. They also specialize in saltwater fish and corals. https://www.oceangallery22.com/

If you are looking to bring a ball python into your family, please consider a reptile rescue, reputable breeder, or a local reptile store that works with reputable breeders. Bringing any reptile into your home is a lifelong commitment.

All photos taken by David Kenny apart from P. 5: Shumba138 (nested image); P. 32: Michael Anderson and Madison Kenny

Ball pythons are nonvenomous snakes that get their name because they will coil into a ball if they get scared, stressed, or just want to feel secure. Their scientific name, *Python regius*, means royal python. (Some believe this is because royalty, such as Cleopatra, queen/pharaoh of Egypt, would wear these snakes like jewelry.)

African rock python

Ball pythons are native to Africa, and they are the smallest African python species. (African rock pythons are the largest.) In the wild, ball pythons live south of the Saharan Desert in swamps, savannahs, marshes, rainforests, and grasslands.

Snakes, including ball pythons, are reptiles. Reptiles rely on the environment to control their body temperature. (They're often called "cold-blooded," though poikilothermic is a technical term that biologists use.)

While ball pythons will bask in the sunlight in the wild, they spend much time in hiding spots and underground in burrows. They are a terrestrial snake species, meaning they are ground-dwellers even though they have the ability to climb rocks and tree branches to explore and hunt.

Ball pythons have become popular as pets given their overall calm and docile nature, plus they are a manageable size. As adults, their average length is about 3 to 5 feet (around 1 to 1.5 meters). Females tend to be larger.

In captivity, ball pythons have specific needs to stay healthy, including enrichment to keep them mentally stimulated. They especially need proper heat and humidity. Guides and books like *A New Keeper's Guide to Ball Pythons* can provide important insights on proper care and how to set up an enclosure.

Ball pythons are heavy-bodied snakes, meaning they are stout and stocky in comparison to their length. They can weigh between 3 to 5 pounds (1.4 kg to 2.27 kg). Their heads are pear-shaped, and they tend to have thin necks as well as tails that are short for their body length.

These snakes are thick due to their strong muscles. Like other kinds of pythons, ball pythons are constrictors. They coil around prey and then squeeze before swallowing their meal whole.

Ball pythons do not pose a threat to people. They might bite in defense if they feel threatened, or if they happen to mistake someone for food. Their teeth are small and short—perfect for gripping prey before swallowing, never chewing once.

Unlike human teeth, snake teeth will fall out and be replaced regularly throughout their lives. In the wild, ball pythons hunt at night (nocturnal), eating rodents, reptiles, birds, and amphibians. Pet ball pythons often dine on mice and rats.

Mental groove

Snakes *don't* dislocate their jaws to eat. They have flexible ligaments and tendons. Under a ball python's jaw, you can see a line called a mental groove where the skin and ligaments are super stretchy. Their skull even has a special bone that enables them to open their mouth wide!

Snakes don't hear the same way people do, and they don't have the same external ear parts either. They have inner ear structures that hear vibrations, important for hunting prey or avoiding predators. In the wild, ball pythons are preyed upon by large mammals and birds of prey.

Heat pits

Similar to pit vipers and boas, ball pythons have heat-sensing pits that create a "heat-picture" (sort of like a night vision camera) to help them find prey, even in pitch darkness. These pit organs are located along a ball python's upper and sometimes lower lips.

Glottis

Ball pythons smell a different way than humans do. Their forked tongues flick in and out to pick up scents using a smell organ called the Jacobson's organ. They have an opening behind their tongue called a glottis that lets them breathe when they swallow large prey items whole.

It can take ball pythons several days to over a week to digest. (In cold temperatures, their bodies slow down, including digestion.) They can survive for months without eating! Younger snakes need to eat more often than fully grown adults, and they eat smaller prey items until they grow bigger.

Ventral scales cover the underside of a snake to include the belly and the tail. These scales help a snake move! Also on the underside, snakes have a cloaca that passes waste (and is also part of the snake's reproduction system).

Pet ball pythons have been selectively bred to have genetic mutations called morphs. They can be bred to have color, pattern, and scale variations (such as micro-scales or scaleless). Certain morphs may need extra care.

In the wild, ball pythons typically have dark eyes, but some morphs have different eye colors. Their eyes can be blue, green, red/pink, gray, or a mix! Even within the same morph, there can be color and pattern differences.

Ball pythons have cat-like, slit pupils (the center part of the eye) that allow them to see at night when they are active. Their eyes are positioned on the sides of their head facing forward, providing a wide field of vision to see potential threats coming at them.

Apart from scaleless morphs, ball pythons are covered in firm, small scales from the tip of their nose to the end of their tail. They may look slimy, but this is because their scales can be shiny. Ball pythons actually feel sleek and smooth to the touch!

All snakes shed their skin throughout their lives, especially as they grow when they are younger. When this happens, a snake's eyes may appear cloudy or blue as fluid builds between the old and new layers of skin. (This stage is often called "in blue.")

Ideally, snakes should shed their skin in one piece, sort of like a long stocking. Ball pythons need to have high enough humidity to shed properly. Stuck snake shed (including eye caps) can cause discomfort and lead to health problems.

Nostril

Like other kinds of snakes, ball pythons have two nostrils (nares) on the top of their snout, close to their eyes. They breathe through their nostrils and mouth. Smoke, incense, candles, air sprays, chemicals, and more can irritate their sensitive respiratory system.

Ball pythons have two lungs that help them breathe, though their left lung is smaller and less developed. Unlike you, they do not have a diaphragm so they can't cough. In captivity, ball pythons can get respiratory infections from strong smells, dirty enclosures, or problems with the temperature and/or humidity. Exotic veterinarians provide healthcare for ball pythons.

Ball pythons have hundreds of bones that give them strength and flexibility! Vertebrae make up their backbone, and hundreds of ribs protect their organs. While ball pythons are hardy overall, it is important to be careful when handling them and to make sure they don't fall.

A strong and flexible backbone helps ball pythons wrap around prey and to also slither away from the threat of predators. Ball pythons can periscope, or scope for short, by raising their heads high off the ground to look around.

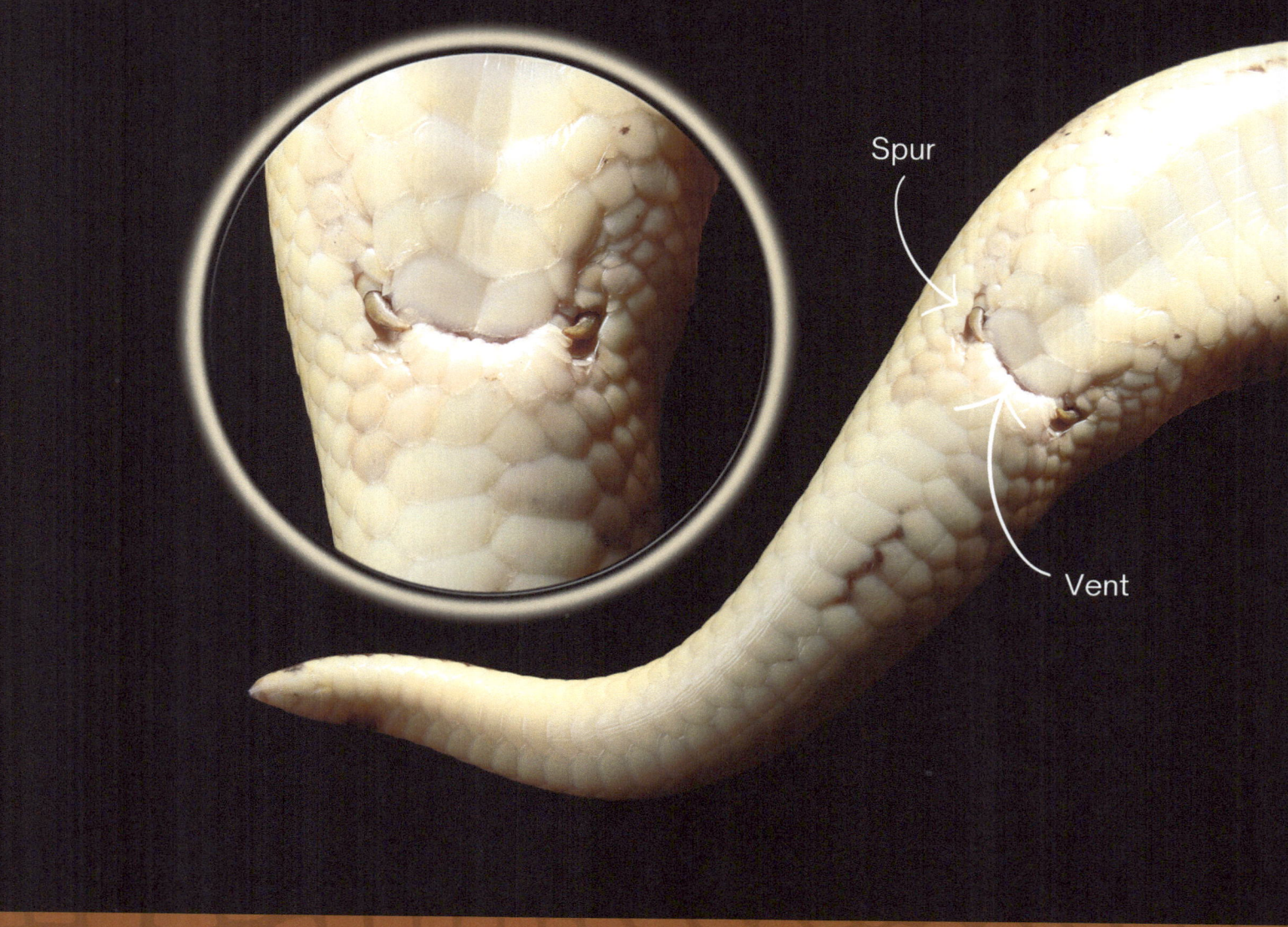

Spur

Vent

Both male and females have spurs that look like claws near their vent (the outside opening that leads to the cloaca). Scientists believe that these were once functional hind legs in the ancestors of ball pythons (called vestigial remnants). Ball pythons use these spurs during mating courtship.

Ball pythons reproduce by laying eggs, about 4 to 12 in a clutch on average. In about two months, viable ball pythons will use an "egg tooth" to make a slit in the egg, popping their heads out to take their first breath of air. They will fully hatch out of the egg about a day or two later. (The "egg tooth" will fall off soon after.)

Research shows that ball pythons are intelligent and have the ability to learn, adapt, and bond socially. Pet ball pythons can recognize their owners, especially if they have their needs met and are shown patience, kindness, and gentleness.

Wild ball pythons live about 10 years on average. They can live over 30 years in captivity with proper care. Ball pythons are one of the most popular snake species given their docile nature, size, hardiness, unique looks, and interesting features!

Jessica Lee Anderson is an award-winning author of over 75 books for young readers including the NAOMI NASH chapter book series and many nonfiction books about reptiles. Jessica loves spending time in nature and exploring the outdoors with her husband, Michael, and their daughter, Ava! You can learn more about Jessica by visiting www.jessicaleeanderson.com.

David Kenny is a photographer from northern New Jersey who enjoys photographing all types of reptiles, amphibians, mammals, and landscapes. His images have been published in numerous books, magazines, calendars and articles. David would like to thank Craig Ost, Marvin Sanchez, Brian Parkhurst, and Bill DiMuccio.

Want to learn more about reptiles? Check out these books:

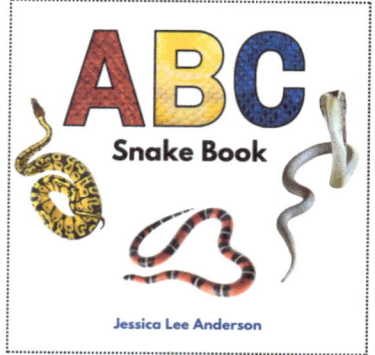

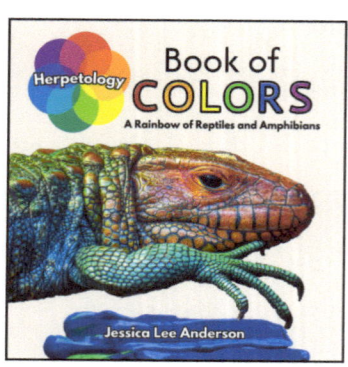

www.ingramcontent.com/pod-product-compliance
Lightning Source LLC
Chambersburg PA
CBHW041436120626
46547CB00002B/247